DANCING IN THE MIST

To Judy & Sheldon,

May you always dance to the sweet music of life.

Amy B K
6/11/04

DANCING IN THE MIST

Bryan B. Kagan

Copyright © 2004 by Bryan B. Kagan.

Library of Congress Number: 2003099514
ISBN : Hardcover 1-4134-3861-X
Softcover 1-4134-3860-1

All rights reserved. No part of this book may be reproduced or transmitted in any form or by any means, electronic or mechanical, including photocopying, recording, or by any information storage and retrieval system, without permission in writing from the copyright owner.

This book was printed in the United States of America.

To order additional copies of this book, contact:
Xlibris Corporation
1-888-795-4274
www.Xlibris.com
Orders@Xlibris.com
22821

CONTENTS

WRITER'S INTRODUCTION	11
ACKNOWLEDGEMENTS	13
LIFE	17
THE REIGN OF BEAUTY	18
THE MOTIONS OF LOVE	19
FRUSTRATION	20
SIMMER	21
AAAH....	22
RETRIBUTION	23
QUICKSAND	24
THE WAIT	25
SOULMATES	26
O'MEO OH MY!	27
IMBALANCE	28
EVOLVING HISTORY	29
GLORY	30
ABRA-CADABRA CANDELABRA	31
GLIMPSES	32
CRUMBS	33
MIRROR MIRROR IN MY MIND	35
NECTOR	36
LITTLE ANGEL, LITTLE GIRL	37
WHEN?	38
PRISM OF A RAINBOW	39
RAPTURE	40
PICNIC IN HEAVEN, ON EARTH	41
IN MY MOTHER'S ARMS	42
ODE TO BLUEBERRIES	43

THE BOOK OF LIFE	44
GENTLE STREAM	45
ETERNAL LIGHT	46
THE MUSIC NEVER STOPS!	47
IN THE BLINK OF AN EYE	48
NOT JUST A KISS	49
NIGHTMARE	50
A PAINTER'S CANVAS	51
GENTLE BRIDEGROOM	52
LIFEBLOOD	53
BALANCE BEAM	54
MANNA	55
THE WAIT!?!?!	56
LIFE AFTER DEATH AFTER LIFE	57
DON'T LET GO	58
WHY WON'T YOU?	59
AROMATHERAPY	60
PRIESTLY BLESSING	61
WITH OUTSTRETCHED ARMS	62
THE PLAYGROUND	63
AFTER ALL IS SAID AND DONE	64
MYSTIC DANCER	65
LITHOGRAPH	66
IT MUST BE THE LIGHT	67
THE POWER OF FLOWERS	68
A FLOWER DANCE	69
THE GAMBLE	70
JONATHAN AND DAVID	71
THE GUARDIAN	72
BUT WHY?????	73
DOUBT	74
THE MOMENT	75
THANKING YOU IN ADVANCE	76
LIFEGUARD??????????	77
PRE-OP	78
JOYFUL LIFE	79

SPARKS	80
NEWBORN	81
NOT AN ONION	82
YOU ARE . . . FOREVER!	83
HOBO	84
THE SACRIFICE	86
DANCING IN THE MIST	87
I DARE NOT BLINK	88
TEARS	89
SHOOTING STAR	90
SYMBIOSIS	91
A PINCH OF REALITY	92
A PINCH OF REALITY!! PART II	93
OUCH!	94
AN EDUCATED CONSUMER, A HEAVENLY PERSPECTIVE	95
MY DEAR BELOVED	96
PASSING OVER	97
FRINGES	98
THE BURNING BUSH	99
STUMBLING STONE	100
AURA	101
SEASONS OF LOVE	102
THE HUSBAND	103
THE PARK BENCH	104
TWO LIGHTS	106
VANTAGE POINT	107
A BRIDGE IN SILHOUETTE	108
BIG DADIO	110
ON THE RUNWAY	111
JUST THINK!	112
DO YOU REMEMBER?	113
FACE TO FACE	114
CLEAR VISION	115
LOVE THAT IS NOT BLIND	116
JUST DANCE!	117

To the One

and Only One

WRITER'S INTRODUCTION

Life is a dance that we perform to the music that touches our souls. It is not always clear where our steps, our choices in life, will lead us. It is as if we are "Dancing In The Mist".

ACKNOWLEDGEMENTS

I am grateful to my dear wife and dance partner, Maggie. Throughout the years you have taught me so much about the basic steps of life, the frame of living and the dancing; you are amazing! Thank you for sharing the dance floor with me and for being such an exceptional mother.

To my children, Jordana, Ben, and Seth. I am uplifted daily by your strength, sensitivity, and spirit; you are constant sources of love, joy and inspiration to me.

To my sister, Michele, for always going the extra mile for me, even in a blizzard. To my brother, Michael, always my hero, making me feel secure knowing that I can always count on you.

To Rabbi Jacob Rubenstein, my teacher, for his enlightening sparkle and for inspiring *The Sacrifice* and *Tears*.

It is a pleasure to acknowledge my friends in the Sephardic Minyan; they are exceptional people and wonderful friends: Abe Dweck who inspired *Priestly Blessing*, Itzhak Nidam, Roger Guigui, Marc Bengualid, Robert Sherr, Roberto Estrugo, David Kelaty, Dr. Moshe Labi, Dr. Meir Asher, Sohiel Daniel, Eli Hezi, Amir Matityahu, Isac Tabib, Shlomo Besharim, Joey Zeitouni, Lee Buchwald, David Bieber, and Israel Teitelbaum.

I want to single out for special mention, Nancy Ivers for inspiring the title, *Dancing in The Mist,* during an office conversation, Brianna V. whose explosive smile in a photograph inspired *Little Angel, Little Girl*, Anaelle G. who inspired *Newborn* via a heavenly dream, Ora and Oren Nidam who inspired *Two Lights*, and Jill Doornick who "needled" me into serenity with acupuncture and inspired *Mystic Dancer*.

To Kate Fairchild, aka "the girl", who always keeps the office running as smoothly, stress free, and efficiently as possible and who uttered a thought, inspiring *Aura*. Your input, dedication, and friendship is greatly appreciated. Its a pleasure and honor to be your friend and to work with you.

To Ana Brito Correia, my friend and art consultant, who designed the cover of this book, contributed art and photographs for *The Reign of Beauty, Quicksand, A Painter's Canvas, The Power of Flowers, Thanking You in Advance, Clear Vision* and *Just Dance!* and who inspired *A Painter's Canvas*. Your artistic eye and insightful perceptions have added color to my life. I am indeed fortunate to be your friend.

For the guidance and love of my dear departed mother, Shirley Smyle Kagan, *Abra-cadabra Candelabra, In My Mother's Arms,* and *Sparks,* and my beloved departed grandfather, Benzion Kagan, *Abra-cadabra Candelabra,* and *Sparks,* I eternally give thanks.

Finally, in memory of my friends, Arthur Breslow z"l and Bertha Sofair z"l, who epitomize *Sparks,* and who left their soulprints in the sands of my heart and mind.

I thank you all.

DANCING IN THE MIST

LIFE

Lonely days, lonely nights
happy days, happy nights,
life is full of sorrows and it's full of joys.
No one really knows or understands
why we act the way we do,
why we feel the way we do.
I guess that's life.
Life is planned out for all of us and we have to go along with it or else.
Or else life is not life,
because life is good with bad,
it's night with day,
it's love with hate,
it's us.
Yes us!
Life would not be if not for us
and we would not be if not for life because that's life.
So if we don't understand how we act, how we feel
then how do we understand life?
Life is too great to comprehend
however you know . . . I know . . . we all know . . . .
life is life and that's that!

1965

THE REIGN OF BEAUTY

Water drips from the overflowing gutter
peeling away petals of beautiful red roses
as raindrops defoliate trees of their most beautiful leaves.
Swept away in the sudden autumn showers,
the colorful petals and leaves drift away forever....

1969

THE MOTIONS OF LOVE

Love, like the seas rolling waves,
lulls one into an abysmal trough.
Rolling, rolling... motions in a doldrum,
hopes and ambitions suspended together beyond reach.
Rising, rising... until riding on cresting white foam,
it crashes down to reality,
splitting rocks and shells...

FRUSTRATION

He gazes up to the moon,
she gazes up beyond.
He looks into her eyes,
while she looks through his.
He would give her his heart,
but she wants more.
He would give her his life,
but that would not be enough.
He wants reassurances from her,
but all he gets are smiles and sighes.
A cool breeze sweeps through his body like a knife cutting,
leaving only a frozen tundra.
He shudders to think what life would be like with her,
or worse, without her.

SIMMER

Exhausted, gasping for air,
he rolls over and stares at her.
Gently stroking aside her hair,
he is overwhelmed by her.
It was only a short time ago
when enraptured by her sweet embrace,
his love began to grow,
his heart began to race.
Was it a dream or was it real
those electric sparks that he would feel?
Could he even begin to measure
all the joy, happiness and pleasure
when pulsating in rhythm with her,
flowing like a river meandering through . . . .
irrigating fallow fields of thought.

AAAH . . . .

You've got that magical mystery
that totally intrigues me.
You! . . . cause my blood to surge
that climaxes when our two bodies merge,
and that entwines our warmth into one
as we love until the rising sun.
Hearing our hedonistic sighes
and seeing our transfixed eyes,
oh my . . . .
It drives me crazy with burning desire
to reach the source of your sweet fire.

RETRIBUTION

Sitting . . . watching the minutes tick by
waiting . . . wondering if she will call.
He cries out for her love but she just sighes.
Praying that someday she'll hear his heart but isn't that folly?
With each passing moment, resolution becomes more determined.
Its growing dark, the sun is setting, tonight again she did not call.
His sweet love of innocence is neglecting him,
but he shall not neglect to repay her.

QUICKSAND

Caught in the quagmire of love,
betrayed by brief moments of passion,
he sinks deeper into the sands of indifference.

THE WAIT

The perfect union,
its existence is no illusion,
so he just sails on the brainwaves of thought
and waits.

SOULMATES

She entered his life
that was filled with emptiness, turmoil and internal strife.
He sensed it, he felt it, he knew it to be true
confirmed by explosions of white and blue
that after a millenia of wait
he was standing face to face with his soulmate.
He gazed into her eyes, the gates of eternity,
travelling through the tunnels of their immortality.
Their awareness grew
as their soul touched anew
flitting and melting together
twirling and swirling into forever
never returning to their previous plane of existence
for they awakened and expanded their spiritual essence
reaching so very high
asking what, when, where, how, and why.
Now he knows that soulmates really do exist,
and that reality will never again be so easily dismissed.
She brought him contentment and fulfillment . . . and let me not
    be remiss
she brought him spiritual bliss.

O'MEO OH MY!

Do you remember? . . . I'll never forget
that very first time when we met.
You overwhelmed my heart as you walked across the room;
mountains shook, the earth quaked, my body trembled, it was a
    sonic boom.

IMBALANCE

Husband and wife,
body and soul joined at the heart.
That's how it is supposed to be,
but unfortunately for all too many
that's not the reality.

EVOLVING HISTORY

A soul's history
is like the seasons of a tree.
Year after year a ring is added to the tree,
while to the soul, lifetime after lifetime is added a new physical body.
They both go through seasonal experiences over and over,
year after year with only slight deviations,
growing . . . growing thicker and taller.
The tree trying to reach into the skies,
the soul trying to reach into heaven.

GLORY

With just an outstretching of Your hand
freedom reverberates throughout the land.
You define power, You define might
and in Your protection and guidance do we delight.
Your ways are unfathomable to all but a few
but Your ways are absolute and always true.

ABRA-CADABRA CANDELABRA

Flickering flames fanning flashbacks,
faces staring back, reflected off of melting candle wax.
Faces glowing brilliantly with light
continuing to illuminate our lives and our moral sight.
Flickering flames shining so bright revealing what was before
and simultaneously revealing the key to the door
that leads to our future.

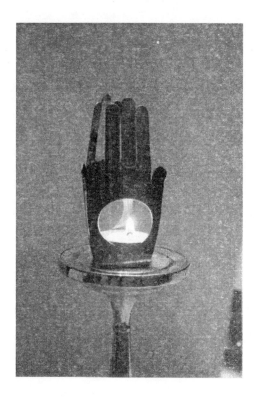

GLIMPSES

Enraptured by the beauty of Your face
my body is entwined with You in a cosmic embrace.
My eyes pierce the barrier of previous lives
as I stare through Your eyes, the windows to my soul;
and my soul like a bird released from its cage
soars up into the sky . . . .
free at last.

CRUMBS

He really thought you loved him when you first wed,
but after all these years, its like he has been kicked in the head.
"Was it wrong to ask for so much
like a desirous look or an ocasional tender touch?
You kept saying it was perceptional, the problem was all mine
because according to you everything was wonderful, for you all was fine."
But he was in emotional pain
and not as you thought sexually insane.
And you deserted him . . . .
He never felt as he should have, enveloped in your love
like a cold hand in winter warmed by a fleece-lined glove.
You only threw him crumbs from the altar of love.

You no longer seem to communicate
and your inaction to respond seems just to seal your fate.
"Because whatever I say, you perceive as an exercise in therapy
which seems to be one sided, meant only for me."
You don't truly listen to him or sincerely take it to heart,
and this stubborness of yours, pierces him mercilessly like a dart.
He apologizes for not being perfect enough for you.
He apologizes for not doing anything right or as good as you could.
He apologizes for not being able to influence you to love him as he
   loved you,
to love him the way he has always asked you to but that you have
   always refused to even attempt.
You never truly comprehended but then again you never really
   tried to comprehend.
He had hoped for so many years that you would change,
and then he hoped for so many years that you would just try,
and now he no longer even hopes.

He could have taken you to a different dimensional plane if you
    had given him your hand,
but you preferred to keep your head hidden comfortably in the sand.
And when you asked for a second chance,
it seems as if you were just toying with him perchance,
because you continued on your way as if nothing was wrong
like Nero fiddling when Rome was burning down.

Shavuot May 1999

MIRROR MIRROR IN MY MIND

Maybe I'm crazy and yet maybe I'm not;
but to me that is how it seems to be
because my feelings tell me one thing
while my heart just cries out for love.
My mind constantly struggles and probably always will
until death . . . when my body will go numb
and I will take leave of myself like a snail that sheds its shell.
Until that day I will just try to live
because maybe I'm crazy and yet maybe I'm not
but still, after all is said and done,
life is indeed beautiful.

NECTOR

Statue of passion
frozen in stone,
embracing life,
embracing love,
floating in the clouds,
dancing in the mist.

LITTLE ANGEL, LITTLE GIRL

Brilliant sparkling eyes
radiating from her soul
an exuberance of life.
Infectious laughter
exploding from her belly
absolute innocence.
Dimpled cheek smiles
erupting from pure joy.
What a blessing!
Grandma's little girl, grandma's little Angel.

WHEN?

When are we going to wake up?
When are we going to wipe away the sleep from our eyes and focus?
When are we going to look at our existence
and consider how the world is defined by us?
When are we going to open our minds
to understand the lightness of a snowflake,
to appreciate the power of a single raindrop,
to realize the inadequacy of words to accurately express our emotions?
When are we going to open our hearts
to understand the tenderness of a touch,
to comprehend the pain of a tear,
to appreciate the power of a smile?
When are going to wake up?

PRISM OF A RAINBOW

Cobblestone pathway leading around the globe
birds singing songs as butterflies flutter by,
flowers in a garden, fragrances in the air
flowers in a garden, blooming in the sun.
Crowds gathering, sitting on park benches in the sun
on cobblestone pathways leading around the globe.

RAPTURE

When You whisper into my ear
Your soft cool breath tickles me;
my heart flutters and my hair stands up on end.
When You whisper into my ear
electrical currents run up and down my spine,
and the twinkle that I think I see in others eyes
is in fact the twinkle in my own eyes which ignites from Your inspiration.
When You whisper into my ear
Your soft cool breath captures me
and all else fades into silence.

PICNIC IN HEAVEN, ON EARTH

I look up towards You, my head cradled in Your lap.
I am spellbound at the break of dawn . . . .
You have my heart,
You have my soul.
You are my strength and my might,
You breathe life into me each and every day and night

I look up towards You, my head cradled in Your lap.
I am entranced in the heat of the midday sun.
Your hands, brushing aside my disheveled hair, stroke my temple and caress my being.
My body rests on lush green carpeting
while my soul levitates to kiss Your sweet lips.

I look up towards You, my head cradled in Your lap.
My eyes, feeling heavy with the setting sun, start to close.
You kiss my eyelids and then my lips
as I fall asleep cradled in the warmth of Your embrace.
You are my heart and my soul.
You are my life.

IN MY MOTHER'S ARMS

Steady rolling waves of love
sculpt hard jagged rocks on a desolate shore
into soft smooth shapes and forms
that slowly emerge out of the receding tide.

ODE TO BLUEBERRIES

A basket full of blueberries
freshly picked, basking in the sun
like plump edible purple pearls,
perfect and priceless.

THE BOOK OF LIFE

Words in a book, letters on a page,
just print,
but the ink breathes life.
It explodes from the flow of Your energy.
Not merely words but emotions.
Not merely letters but passion.
Not merely ink but intensity.

GENTLE STREAM

A stream flowing gently
coursing through the meadows and the fields,
from the mountaintops to the seas,
gently coursing through our lives
fed by the runoff of our tears,
absorbing our hopes and our fears.
A stream flowing gently
coursing through our history
witnessing our past and giving testimony to our future,
watering the gardens and the deserts of this world.
We stand on its banks gazing upon the calm reassuring surface
and see reflected, mirror images.
A stream flowing gently
meandering through our emotions;
our emotions wading in the gently flowing stream of love.

ETERNAL LIGHT

Deep within the flames lie Your essence,
exploding sparks of blinding light
bursting forth with penetrating might.
Flickering flames of truth, love, and compassion,
volcanic eruptions of energy and passion.
Never consumed, never diminished, and never extinguished,
it burns eternally.

THE MUSIC NEVER STOPS!

Can one compare a sparkling diamond to a lump of black coal,
or a granule of sand to a shining smooth pearl?
So how can anyone ever compare Your love to anything else in this world?
The blind never see a sunrise or a sunset but they can describe Your beauty.
The deaf never hear a symphony or a baby's cry but they can describe Your voice.
So how can one describe that special awareness of You,
where every breath is a passionate kiss of life,
and every step taken is a Tango with You?
It is like a moonlit dance where your eyes shine like pearls,
your face sparkles like diamonds,
and I am blind to all else.
It is a romantic moonlit dance where the music never stops!

IN THE BLINK OF AN EYE

The time is so short and soon we will be together.
Then, there will be no more illness nor pain nor sadness.
The limitations of time will cease to have control,
as time itself will have no meaning.
The past, the present and the future will fuse into one and be boundless.

NOT JUST A KISS

The core of my existence was only born when I came to know You,
as I came to love You.
Before then, I was just frolicking in sun drenched fields,
alone and unaware.
Now the sun's rays warm my face
as You walk with me upward along a mountain trail,
and when I fatigue, when my stamina starts to fail,
You encourage me on with a kiss,
a kiss that is not just a kiss but a bouquet of emotions.
Emotions that blossom, invigorate and enlighten.

NIGHTMARE

Dawn breaks dark and dreary,
the sky is without color, just shades of gray.
Leafless trees stand naked,
empty of birds singing their morning serenades.
The air is choking, polluted by automotive exhaust fumes.
The radiant glow of Your essence is absent.
There are no angels to sing Your words.
There is no You to hug me in warm serenity.
It can't be happening, it must be a nightmare.

A PAINTER'S CANVAS

Color is just color unless you "see" it.
Poems are just words unless you "sense" it.
Love is just an expression unless you "feel" it.
Feeling is passion.
Passion is absorbing.
Pain comes, it lasts just long enough for the heart to stop, for the heart to hurt.
Love comes, it lasts just long enough for the heart to pause, for the heart to live.
They are but feelings that like a bowl of paint of blended colors
reflect rays of color off a painted canvas
and evoke the passion and emotions that never fade.

GENTLE BRIDEGROOM

The reality was such as he awoke that day,
that this was going to be an especially meaningful day.
In the morning as he observed his reflection in the mirror,
he saw through his eyes into his pounding heart that there was no one dearer
than the one who brought him the gentle Gift of Life.
With the fervor of a franticly fumbling bridegroom, he dressed.
With the exhiliaration of a passionate bridegroom, he ran to meet her,
to glow in her radiant face,
to sway in rhythm with her sweet melodic voice,
just to be in her presence.
He was like an excited bridegroom, anticipating their very first time together,
but this wasn't the first time . . . because it happens each and every time.
It happens each and every time he approaches her
to accept her gentle Gift of Life and to offer her in return his gentle Gift of Love.

LIFEBLOOD

Coursing daily through my beating heart
supplying energy and warmth,
You are the blood that oxygenates my entire body.
You are the blood that gives me life.

BALANCE BEAM

Walking the line
awaiting a heavenly sign,
but unfortunately not with the same agility as a feline,
all the same, just trying to toe the line.

MANNA

The emptiness of not being in Your embrace,
of not hearing Your voice, of not seeing Your face
makes one second feel like a day, a minute like a month,
an hour like a year and a day . . . like eternity.
Some could easily go through life happy and totally unaware.
For them, time could just simply pass by
until their River of Life runs dry.
Nothing would be perceived as deficient, nothing lacking,
because they've never tasted manna, they've never tasted heaven.
For them, life seems full.
But once heaven is tasted,
life is only full when fulfilled by You,
otherwise one is walking through life without a heart, just with a
   lonely soul.

THE WAIT!?!?!

Do you believe with complete faith that he will come,
or to your fears and doubt will you succumb?
After all this time, it must be difficult hoping and waiting
while the clarity of the vision seems to be constantly fading.
But after all this time, can you still feel it?
Do you still sense it?
Although I don't know precisely the arrival date,
I am sure that he will come even if he tarries or is a little late.
But do you still have the depth of faith and patience to wait?

LIFE AFTER DEATH AFTER LIFE

Living our lives in our own little world,
incubating in our own little universe
until it starts to crack
which enables our soul to break out,
to be free . . . .
to escape from the restricting confines of this world's shell.

DON'T LET GO

You held him so close
that he felt Your heart beating inside of him.
This must be heaven!

WHY WON'T YOU?

Screaming in pain during the Roman Crucifixion,
writhing in agony during the Spanish Inquisition,
shivering in fear when the English issued their Edict of Expulsion,
convulsing in Hell when the Nazis implemented their Final Solution,
languishing in silence when the Communists attempted spiritual extermination,
drowning in assimilation in the freedoms of western civilization,
stunned and all alone in global isolation in the aftermath of a terrorist suicide mission,
. . . we are in shock!
Why won't You show your face?

AROMATHERAPY

Your eyes are the flames of fire
that slowly bring my simmering passion to a boil.
Your tender touch stirs up the essence of my soul
like a spoon stirs up the vegetables and meat in a stew.
You are the spice, that when added, imparts a special flavor
and my existence is wonderfully delicious.
The hearth is filled with Your heavenly aroma
and my heart beats lovingly enveloped in the gentleness of Your aura.
You are the expression of my love
and I am nothing but an extension of You.

PRIESTLY BLESSING

Standing erect with eyes closed, facing the Source,
hearing the crescendo of an approaching tide,
he raises his arms and is immediately transformed into a swirling
 particle of white light . . . suspended . . . .
Eyes open to find himself floating within a billowy white fluff of
 cloud . . . hovering . . . .
And then suddenly he is transformed back into a cresting wave of
 white foam
that abruptly carries him back to the physical shore.
Exhiliarated, he arises from the sand smiling.
He finally caught the "wave", he finally body surfed.

WITH OUTSTRETCHED ARMS

The power of Your touch extends even to my dreams.
Whenever and wherever I see You,
even when my eyes are closed,
whenever I even just think of You,
I melt like ice
and flow into Your infinite aura.
You touch me without the use of arms
but with an expansion of mind and soul.
You are my energy.

THE PLAYGROUND

The snow has melted,
the sun is shining,
the grass is greening,
the birds are chirping
as excited children run to explore their playground of imagination.
Their feet never touch the ground;
like angels, they seem to float on the clouds of heaven, playing.
With their universe ever expanding,
they swing higher and higher and higher on the stars
catapulted by the push of previous generations.

AFTER ALL IS SAID AND DONE

I just want to fall asleep in Your arms,
feeling Your soft breath in my ears
as You sing to me a lullaby.
I just want to close my eyes
knowing that You are smiling back at me
holding me close to Your heart
protecting me from the cold night air.
In the end, that is all I really want.

MYSTIC DANCER

Stepping through life
learning the basics
practicing the steps
perfecting the frame
listening to the music
feeling it
absorbing it
embracing it
living it
loving it
going through life,
Dancing in the mist.

LITHOGRAPH

An angel flew down from heaven to kiss me
but missed my lips;
she kissed my heart instead
and before I even understood what I saw,
my eyes welled up in tears,
for the glow of heaven followed her.

IT MUST BE THE LIGHT

Out of the depths of darkness it came to be
atoms and molecules continually swaying in rhapsody
back and forth to Your heavenly melody.
Your music never fades off into silence
it just continues to play as it always has since pre-existence.
Goosebumps erupt on my soul to the sensual touch of Your verbal caress,
blinding explosions of rainbow colors illuminate perception to my eyesight.
There is no beginning, there is no end, there is only a continuum of Your light.
The past, the future and the present all exist as one in Your presence.
There is no limit, there is no boundary only an infinitely flowing expanse
where all life is touched by Your spirit and infused with Your love
because there is no beginning, there is no end, there is only You.

THE POWER OF FLOWERS

As you walk through earthly gardens
do you ever ponder the flowers creation?
It doesn't matter if you look at them with your naked eye or even
    under a microscopic lens.
They stand tall and fragile, temporal monuments of inspiration,
that like radio transmitters have been for eons emitting beacons of beauty.
The richness of their color resonates with the heartbeat of mankind.
Their fragrances waft sensually into our nostrils and fills our minds,
then lulls our spirit to the seminal fields of our innocence and purity
where the boundaries are defined by tulips.
"Two lips" that kiss our eyes and flirt with our imagination.

A FLOWER DANCE

A flower needs to be appreciated,
it needs love and attention as much as water and sun.
Some people, aware of their preciousness, watch them dance,
how they form, how they grow, how they seem to reach for the heavens.
A flower stands in naked beauty waiting... until someone "sees" it,
and then it blooms... filling a life;
that is its purposeful dance.
Its unique hues color the heart
and touches ever so sweetly the soul.

THE GAMBLE

Poking his head out to see if it is safe, to see if the coast is clear,
listening intently for any sounds that might awaken his deafened ear,
he cautiously steps out into a changing gust of wind.
Momentarily thrown off balance as if slipping on ice,
momentarily thrown off balance as if on a craps table, bouncing
    and rolling like thrown dice,
he comes to rest on a pasture of plush green felt
and all of his paralyzing hesitations, and all of his freezing fears melt.

JONATHAN AND DAVID

In all of recorded world history
there was never a relationship of such intensity.
Two souls who stand as a testament to unselfish friendship and love.
Two friends that bonded, loyal to each other;
as if they were weaned by the very same mother.
Two friends like brothers, a young shepherd was one,
the other was the reigning King's beloved son.
Thieves in the night could have robbed them blind
but never would their love and friendship be stolen from their
    collective mind.
One day however, through a heavenly blue sky, an arrow flew
and when it landed, both of them knew
for the location of the arrow's landing was a prearranged cue.
It was so difficult for them that day to find the right words to say;
so they hugged goodbye, took a final look, turned and just simply
    walked away.
But their story enriches mankind's conscious memory
for the flame of their friendship and love still illuminates today so
    brightly and intensely.

THE GUARDIAN

Do you ever doubt, do you ever fear
that you are all alone, that there is nothing else out there?
At night, do you have faith that in the morning the sun will again rise?,
so why is it so difficult to believe in what you can only feel and not
    see with your naked eyes?
You should never doubt nor ever fear
for He is always there,
in the daylight and into twilight
under the moon light and even on a cloudy night,
standing in the freezing winter snow and under the summer sun's
    sweltering heat,
withstanding driving rain, pounding hail, fog and sleet.
He slumbers not as He watches over you in health and sickness,
as He watches over you in sorrow and in happiness.
You should never doubt nor ever fear that you are all alone
for the Guardian is always there . . . and always will be.
His watch is endless!

BUT WHY?????

Why do You look at me the way You do?
Why do You listen to me the way that You do?
How is it that You know my heart,
      knowing what I'll feel, what I'll say, what I'll do?
How do You touch me to the depth of my very soul,
      hugging me the way You do?
Why do You love me the way You do?
It is hidden from me, I don't even have a clue,
but I feel like a rock at the base of a waterfall
as the waters of emotion cascade over my body.
But why do You love me the way that You do?
Perhaps because You love me the way that I love You!

DOUBT

Sharp serrated knife of doubt
surgically slicing away slivers of heart.
Is this a perceptional overanalysis
or could it be a death kiss?

THE MOMENT

He waits so patiently
even though the wait is so long and difficult.
He waits all alone, by himself
waiting for that moment which seems to last but a second.
He waits for that very moment when his feet take leave of the ground
and he elevates like an angel . . . kissing life . . . .
but then gravity reclaims its physical possessions.
Once again his spirit is grounded, his body weighted down
so that he is only capable of contemplating flight.
Still he waits so patiently for the time when the ground will be endless sky,
the kiss will be eternal and the "wait" will have seemed only like a split second.

THANKING YOU IN ADVANCE

Driving on the highway of life,
looking up into the sky
seeing fluffy, billowy pillows of clouds
that You have arranged to cushion our fall
when the world is turned upside down.
We thank you.

LIFEGUARD?????????.

He was drowning, crying out
but she just stood motionless on shore, painting her nails.
He submerged once . . . coming up fighting like a bear . . . gasping for air.
He submerged again . . . coming up hands grasping kelp . . . screaming for help.
He submerged once more but never came back up this time,
her nails finally dried . . . and she became aware of the water's smooth lacquered finish.

PRE-OP

Blinded by the intense light,
searing bright spots of white,
I am unable to look straight ahead or to keep my eyes open.
But if I turn my head off to the side,
there, right before my eyes I see You smiling,
standing tall with a glowing face
basking within a reflective halo of heavenly light,
of compassion, understanding, goodness, mercy and love.
And if I close my eyes, I do not walk blindly in darkness
for through the sheer curtains of my eyelids
I see Your form in full glory before me.

JOYFUL LIFE

Joy is seeing You everyday . . . smiling.
Joy is telling You everyday . . . "I love You" and hearing it back.
Joy is feeling my heart pounding whenever I reach out to touch You and feeling embraced back.
Joy is hearing Your voice full of passion and love for me.
Joy is being touched everywhere by Your eyes.
Joy is knowing that my love for You will never die nor Yours for me.
Joy is just opening my eyes to "see".

SPARKS

Celestial sparks sizzle just seconds
but stimulate a lifetime.

NEWBORN

The sights of seraphim singing while she played cymbals in their symphony are seared into the subconscious of her soul.
The rhythmic vibrations of their songs strum the fibers of her spirit.
Slowly she slides from heavenly existence escorted by serenading angels into the waiting arms of smiling parents whose gleaming eyes resonate to the vibration of celestial song.
A sparkling sapphire, she is securely set in family surrounded by baguettes of love.

NOT AN ONION

He thought that he understood
but his ignorance was a thick hood.
He was sitting in the kitchen preparing for a banquet;
tears flowed freely as he peeled an onion.
Layer by layer he stripped away each subsequent layer
to reveal after the removal of the last layer nothing but emptiness.
That revelation shook his understanding and humbled him
for he was sitting in the kitchen of heaven peeling away the layers
not of an onion but of his soul.

YOU ARE ... FOREVER!

Fortunate am I to have come to know You
for I am blessed, feeling the depth of Your love.
Sadly too many drift through life
without being touched or themselves touching.
Their words are just sounds with no meaning
but Your words are filled with the nectar of life whose sweet juices
    quench my thirst.
Seasons come and go but You remain true.
When I see You ... when I feel You,
even though my body is ravaged by the passage of time,
once again I become that innocent little boy frolicking in fields of
    tall grass,
running along the river's edge holding Your hand, exploring
while You shine on me, igniting a spark, launching me into the heavens.
How fortunate I will have been when my energy fails and my heart
    falls into silence
for You have been my existence.

HOBO

With a jolt, he awakened thinking that the train was disengaging,
    that the coupling was loose,
but it was just the rattling motion of an old rickety caboose.
He knew that stealing a ride on the empty freight train was a crime
but he was penniless, he didn't even have a dime.
And now regaining consciousness from his heavenly drunken stupor
he looked around the empty car, he couldn't have felt any lonlier.
His eyelids were crusted partially closed so that he could hardly
    focus his eyes,
and his lips sealed with dryness, muffled his pitiful cries.
He was stressed out and it just didn't seem fair;
the anxiety paralyzed him, he even had difficulty breathing the air.
So he rested one hand over his pounding heart
and set the thumb of his other hand on his forehead . . . .

The train kept moving day and night over the uneven terrain,
slowly winding along on the rails through sleet, snow, drought
    and rain.
The stinging desert wind tattered his clothes, baring his scarred skin,
and tore apart his satchel blowing away all the material possessions
    that were within.
Standing naked and alone he wondered if he would ever reach the
    final destination
or be found out and thrown off at the very next station? . . . .

But the train continued moving at its predetermined pace
while the wind, like dermabrasion, relentlessly slapped his body
    and face,
slowly smoothing his scars and polishing his soul . . . .
When finally the train pulled into the last station,
when his journey finally came to a conclusion,
he was still standing completely naked.
But he was wealthy beyond compare,
because the most valuable and precious possessions
were those protected in his heart and guarded by his soul.
He stretched out his arms and opened his palms wide as he stepped
    off the train;
he was not alone, just anticipating the embrace.

THE SACRIFICE

It is totally illogical, it just doesn't make sense,
unfortunately the key to its understanding is hidden behind a fence.
Its comprehension, protected by a mental minefield,
is for all intents and purposes securely sealed.
The majority of us don't even have a clue,
it is penetrable to a very select few.
But it doesn't really matter what they think or feel,
if they perceive it as a dream or perhaps sense that it is indeed real
because the truth of all reality, the essence of all dreams is You.

DANCING IN THE MIST

Life is a dance.
    The steps we take,
        our tempo,
            and our frame
                are all determined by the music that we hear
                    which may not always be distinct or clear.
We move our body to what we perceive as the beat
        not exactly sure what shape or form our dance will take.
             We move across the floor, hesitant and unsure in our steps;
                dancing as if in a dense fog
                      not sure how we will eventually be judged when
                        the music stops.

I DARE NOT BLINK

Through a crack in a windowsill on a cold winter night
a warm breeze penetrates and whispers throughout the house.
Goosebumps explode on my arms and back like a succession of
    volcanic eruptions,
while an awareness of a calming presence is felt within swirling about.
Who is this youthful windswept spirit in the hearth?
Sent from heaven, she shimmers like a stream in sunlight, flowing
    with boundless energy.
She is the white light of existence that diverges through the prism
    of my eyes
into a rainbow of emotions, understanding and patience.

TEARS

Tears of the father, tears of the son
sharing a common vision, spiritually vibrating in unison.
Together they approached the sacrificial altar of love
while the angels wept in the heavens above.
A misperceived instruction was all that it took,
the world convulsed, then held its breath,
its very existence was teetering . . . between life and death.
But the faith of the father never wavered, his hand never shook;
the faith of the son never vacillated as he stretched his neck bare,
he was prepared, he was ready to ascend as an offering up into the air.
Transfering the vision as if in a relay race
the tears of the father, like a baton, flowed freely down his aged face
passing into the receptive eyes of his heavenbound youthful son.
Tears of the father, tears of the son
sharing a vision, building an eternal foundation.

SHOOTING STAR

Why does every day have to be such a struggle?
Why can't we just sit at home, relax, read, hug and snuggle?
Why don't we awaken calm and at peace in the Garden of Eden,
instead of anxious and irritated by the world's cacophonous din?
Why is the meaning of life so mysterious and difficult to discern?
I guess we are not ready yet, there's just too much more for us to learn.
But who will teach, who will inspire
pushing us to reach ever higher and higher?
Who will stoke the fire to ignite our desire
to fill our minds with the fragrance of the Essence?
Perhaps a star shooting across a darkened sky.

SYMBIOSIS

Pour out your heart to Me
and I will return an open ear.
Pour out your pain and hurt to Me
and I will return My love.
Empty the anguish from your soul
and I will once again make you whole.

A PINCH OF REALITY

Why did you pinch so hard?
Why did your words have to be so harsh, your tone so mean?
Was it because you were hurting and upset?
Was it because I didn't show My face to you
when you wanted Me to?
Was it because I didn't answer you
when you were expecting me to?
At any rate, it was a pinch of reality
and now unfortunately the curtain of separation has started to descend,
and My presence is one step behind it.
You may not be able to see Me again
but I will always be there watching over you,
wherever your path leads you, whatever choices you make,
and I will always love you as I have always loved you . . . forever.

A PINCH OF REALITY!!
PART II

What seemed like a curtain was in fact a door,
a metal frame fire door.
It separated two worlds.
He stood motionless and waited on one side
in a dark, damp, dreary cellar of lifelessness.
But then he peered through a small window in the door
and saw into the other side,
an inviting, warm, brightly lit hall of color, life and cheerfulness.
There he saw a smiling apparition with fluttering wings, floating.
She was waiting for his face to appear in the window
and once acknowledged, she approached, flowing gently towards
    the door,
her feet not even touching the floor.
She approached slowly, capturing his attention
captivating his focus and his concentration.
A wave of warmth and love rushed the corners of the door, slowly
    pushing it open
and like the ocean tide, drew him back into the bosom of life;
then the door closed shut forever behind him.

OUCH!

This world within which we live is an illusion,
it exists only to foster confusion.
The world beyond however, is the reality,
a constant truth that extends forever into eternity.
Only a few can perceive it.
Only a few will contemplate it
because at times there is pain and at times joy when trying to
    bridge them
but that is the reality of the illusion,
that is the illusion of the reality.

AN EDUCATED CONSUMER, A HEAVENLY PERSPECTIVE

The store room is fully packed,
the shelves completely stacked.
Wide open eyes dare not blink for fear of missing all the exotic choices
 and enticingly displayed tasty delicacies
that have been promoted by serpentine-like aggressive advertising
 strategies.
But as you walk up and down the aisles of life, just remember
every item that you take, will be priced at the check-out counter
 by the register scanner.
So shop wisely!
An educated consumer realizes that no one ever gets out of this
 worldly grocery store on their way to heaven without paying
 the full price of what is in their shopping cart.

MY DEAR BELOVED

Oh, how I have missed you!
It seems like it has been such a very long time
and I can't wait to see you again.
Unfortunately we never seem to spend enough time together
but I think about you day and night.
As I approach you now, the pitter patter in my heart intensifies,
and my stomach flutters with butterflies.
I explode with primal emotions
for you detonate my deepest passions.
I will wrap my arms around you and nuzzle at your neck
inhaling your fragrance which fills me with peaceful completeness.
You satiate my hunger with your lips,
and quench my thirst with your honey nectar kisses.
My fingers will run through your hair and my hands will explore
    your shape.
Our bodies will touch while my eyes penetrate . . . absorbing your
    uniqueness.
You are the love of my youthful innocence,
and the love of my approaching senescence.
You are the love of my life!

PASSING OVER

Finally in your arms again
like a baby chick under the wings of its mother hen,
warm and secure, loved and at peace.

FRINGES

From the four corners of the earth
fringes hang as on the garments of mankind.
Threads that wrap around the globe
tieing together the four seasons of the year which unite in life and
   in love
Threads that wrap around the heart
tieing together four chambers uniting the body and maintaining
   life.

THE BURNING BUSH

Passion, like the burning bush,
burns with an intense flaming fire
but is not consumed.

STUMBLING STONE

A stubborn stone blocks his path,
it is set in the middle of the road preventing his passage.
With all of his strength, over days, weeks, months and years he struggles
and continually stubs his toes, sprains his ankles and even sometimes
   throws out his back
but still he is unable to move the stone.
It does not budge.
His sweat collects into a moat surrounding the stone but fails to
   loosen up the rockbed.
Drop by drop, the tears of his pain and sadness fall but fail to
   make a groove,
they fail to erode a slight indentation on the cool smooth surface
   of the stone.
Instead they just bounce off and the salty tears sting his skin and
   cause his heart to contract.
Frustrated and exhausted, he turns away from that path.

AURA

What is an aura????????
but the perfume of one's soul,
and the garden of my life is infused with your sweet fragrance.

SEASONS OF LOVE

Love when vibrant, erupts like a volcano with explosions of life.
Lava flows with exquisite color and intense heat;
nothing can stand in its way.
But then over time, the lava cools and slowly hardens.
It was breathtaking when active, but then you no longer see it.
Where once was fire, where once was flowing lava has become now
    just cool, hard rock,
and the volcanic eruption that you saw and felt is just a memory in
    your mind.

THE HUSBAND

Do you realize how much he loves you
even though he he doesn't verbally say so?
But you should know
that he says it in the things that he does for you.
He is like the diamond in your ring that sparkles and shines in the
    sunlight,
clear, full of color, flawless and bright
all because of you, for you are his sunlight.

THE PARK BENCH

Sitting on a park bench, friends, deep in thought and conversation,
discussing life and all of its tribulations,
trying to understand, trying to find meaning
gathering in, analyzing, savoring life's gleanings.
Asking what is it really all about?
Why do people mechanically hurry and run about?
Why do some wallow in self pity, and others languish in self doubt?
Why are some happy and content, screaming with delight an orgasmic shout
while others are confused and lost, paralyzed with a frozen facial pout?
What is it all about? Why?
Why do nations behave like children, fighting and hating and encouraging violence
when it is just futile, when it just doesn't make any sense.
Why do nations attempt to dominate others as their God given burden,
a right that will fail, on that you can be certain.
Why can't they just clear the air . . . and share
their knowledge of land, religion, culture, family and memories
acknowledging the differences but embracing their similarities.
Why can't they be like friends sitting on a park bench, deep in thought and conversation,
their feet firmly set on the ground,
their minds soaring like seagulls over Long Island Sound,
just trying to understand, just trying to find the solution.
In truth however, there may not be a single answer only more questions
but that may be the answer for in the questioning lies the lessons.

TWO LIGHTS

With the sound of cracking glass, this fragile universe came to attention;
all the laws of physics were suddenly held in suspension.
There was no movement of air
and even passing golfers stopped to stare.
The devil himself tried to stoke the fire in the furnace of hell
but the heat of their passion overwhelmed him like an ocean swell,
silencing him and extinguishing his fire.
Simultaneously, out of the heavens came the sounds of minstrels
 playing the lyre.
Birds were flying escort as angels serenaded with love songs;
clouds were providing a protective canopy as flowers swayed,
 dancing seductively.
The radiant bride illuminated the aisle as her groom waited anxiously.
Two lights, one shining and one sparkling, converged on a path
 and then emerged as one.
The heavens cracked open with a smile at that very exact moment
 and blew a kiss
sealing a blessing of enduring devotion and eternal bliss.
And then all of a sudden the air moved and someone started to cough,
traffic once again became congested and golfers started teeing off;
it became just another ordinary day . . . except for those who were
 there,
except for those who witnessed the procession of brilliant lights.

July 6, 2003

VANTAGE POINT

He was just walking the line, living on the edge
until he leaned over and looked out over the window's ledge.
From this vantage point he saw his life and wept, "Where did all the time go?".
Sadly he came to realize that he just didn't know.
For far too many years his mind had been numbed by stress and pain and he didn't remember
when the intense raging fire of his youth was reduced to a single smoldering ember.
But a gentle breeze blew, stoking the ember revealing a flickering spark.
From his vantage point he saw and wept because in that flickering spark lay hope
and hope is the eternal light that touches the soul escorting it into eternity.

A BRIDGE IN SILHOUETTE

Somewhere . . . between here and there,
there is a bridge crossing over a gentle stream . . . or a mountainous ravine.
It matters not how small or how great the divide
the bridge connects land.

Sometime . . . between now and then,
there is a bridge crossing over a flowing continuum.
It matters not how long or how short the interval
the bridge connects day to daybreak.
The bridge connects time

Some realm . . . between the physical and the metaphysical
there is a bridge crossing over . . . .
It matters not in what dimension one is in
the bridge connects life to afterlife.
The bridge connects self.

Some . . . who are between living and lived
never realize that they are on a bridge crossing over.
It matters
for the bridge connects understanding, comprehension, and
    knowledge to wisdom.
It connects living to love and loving to life.

A bridge crosses over a gentle stream
as white ducks gracefully glide like angels from shore to shore.
Children throw crumbs of food to the ducks as they always have
everywhere and anywhere . . . wherever and whenever . . . throughout
    all the ages . . . .
They are silhouettes on a bridge.

BIG DADIO

What kind of father are You?
Why are You hiding from us? Where are You?
Why do You just sit back on Your throne like a king,
detached and removed, not seeming to care about anything?
Your children have looked to You for guidance after experiencing
 hardships and hate
but You just turn Your head away and close Your eyes preferring
 to sit and wait.
For what?!?! What are You waiting for????????!
What kind of example are You setting that we should emulate
when You dangle us as if we are fish bait.
We don't "really" know what you mean,
but then You prefer to remain hidden, obscure and unseen.
Your promises are yet fulfilled empty . . . talk is cheap;
our spirits are wanting but Your answering machine is full . . .
 beep . . . beep . . . beep.
Mankind awaits!!!!!!!!!!!!!!!!!!!!!!
Start being the Father You are supposed to be!

ON THE RUNWAY

Life is a continuum.
It flows like an eternal fashion show
where the model walks down the runway
returning each time in different clothes
like a soul reincarnating . . . .

JUST THINK!

By what mechanism does it operate?
It can't be just a matter of fate
when sons look like their fathers
or daugthers like their mothers
sharing gait patterns, bone structure, personalities,
facial expressions, vocal enunciations,
height, qualities of hair and the color of their eyes.
Just as physical genes are passed from one generation to the next,
couldn't there be spiritual "genes" that are transmitted from one
    lifetime to the next?
Think about it—push open the door....
just think about it alittle bit more.
What is the essence of a man at his end?
He is but a soul that like a fruit at the end of the harvest
germinated from a seed of the same fruit from a previous season
and that will transmit his seed into the next planting season.
Keep thinking about it just alittle bit more;
keep pushing open that door.
If toxic wastes, chemical preservatives and radiation
can affect the physical DNA causing disease and genetic mutation,
then can not also sin
throw spiritual DNA into a tailspin?
But not all the physical changes are irreversible
especially if the irritations cease, if they are removable,
so shouldn't also repentance
spark a remission or possibly even a spiritual deliverance?
Just think!

DO YOU REMEMBER?

They say all is forgotten at the moment of birth,
when the angels touch our lips, when we return to earth.
But yet some go through life searching, questioning, trying to find
the "essence".
They seem to experience a nostalgic sense of heavenly well being
wherever they go by hearing, by smelling, and by seeing
while most just look at them thinking they are wasting their time
pursuing nonsense.
So why is it that they didn't forget?
Why are they intuitively aware of an "essence"?
Maybe the angels just didn't touch them hard enough.

FACE TO FACE

My body starts to shake,
my hand trembles as it scribbles words of apology on tearsoaked paper.
Did You think I forgot about You, that I didn't care?
Did You think I was so busy and preoccupied that You weren't an
    integral part of me?
I'm sorry, please don't ever doubt me
because before I was even born until after I am long gone
I am Yours.
My heart calibrates to the rhythm of Your pulse.
Your magnetism draws me,
Your electricity empowers me.
I am inside, Face to Face, feeling You, knowing You
and my soul reflects out from the depths of Your eyes.
By birth and by choice You are the Rock of my Salvation.

CLEAR VISION

I was a butterfly like a princess in the sky,
flying with passion and energized by the touch of purity in the air.
I landed on a paradise of love which to the unknown world was
   just an empty park bench.
The feeling was one of overall warmth.
Birds were singing, it was a sunny day.
The sound of a nearby waterfall was sweet to my ears.
I knew that this was life
and I was passionately connected to eternity.

LOVE THAT IS NOT BLIND

Looking up I wonder where You are
and even though I don't see You, it doesn't mean that You aren't there.
The twinkling star up in the darkened skies
is the same that sparkles in my eyes.
You are the bright shining light that exists as heaven;
You are the same bright shining light that illuminates my heart.

JUST DANCE!

Learning the basics, steps and frame
realizing that everyone has their unique style, no one dances the same.
It doesn't really matter if some dance barefoot while others dance
   in formal attire
because the purpose of life is to always just dance with passion and fire
so that the footprints of the steps we make
leave imprints in the sands of time.